Letters for Reluctant Leaders
(& Eager Ones Too)

Ruth Lichtenberger

Eleven Studies on 1 & 2 Timothy

InterVarsity Press
Downers Grove
Illinois 60515

InterVarsity Press is the book-publishing
division of Inter-Varsity Christian
Fellowship, a student movement active on
campus at hundreds of universities,
colleges and schools of nursing.
For information about local and regional
activities, write IVCF, 233 Langdon St.,
Madison, WI 53703.

Distributed in Canada through
InterVarsity Press, 1875 Leslie St., Unit 10,
Don Mills, Ontario M3B 2M5, Canada.

ISBN 0-87784-303-1

Printed in the United States of America

Introduction

You're human.

Are you a leader? You're still human.

Leaders have problems like everyone. Some come from within (weaknesses of personality, ability or body) and some from without (circumstances, other people and so on). If God has put you in a place of leadership, realize that he never said you'd be problem free. He did promise help in working through the problems that will inevitably come. As Paul wrote Timothy, "Indeed all who desire to live a godly life in Christ Jesus will be persecuted" (2 Tim. 3:12).

Timothy. Timothy was a leader. Paul left him in Ephesus to handle certain difficulties in the church (1 Tim. 1:3) which he had begun there but which soon faced great opposition from outside (see Acts 19—20). Within the church, too, were false teachers and problems in church order. Timothy was just the man for the job. He might have become a Christian as a result of Paul's direct ministry (1 Cor. 4:17; 2 Tim. 1:2). He had traveled with Paul on his missionary journeys (Acts 16: 1-5; 17:10-15; 20:1-5). He had been a trusted apostolic delegate to Thessalonica and Corinth (1 Thess. 3:1-3; 1 Cor. 4:17). He had received a commission to minister by the laying on of hands (1 Tim. 4:14; 2 Tim. 1:6). In fact Paul went so far as to say, "I have no one like him" (Phil. 2:19-24).

Or was he just the man? He was young and would have to face some difficulty in holding the respect of those he was placed over (1 Tim. 4:12; 1 Cor. 16:10-11). He was prone to sickness (1 Tim. 5:23). Lastly, he seemed to lack assertiveness and self-confidence (2 Tim. 1:7-8). Hardly the ideal leader. Yet God had called him to the task.

In these letters to Timothy, Paul sought to encourage and instruct this young leader in three main areas: (1) the task of organizing the church; (2) the need to maintain pure doctrine (Paul uses the words *truth, faith, gospel* and *doctrine* to mean the whole body of truth God has revealed); and (3) the fight to live as a Christian leader should—with courage and holiness. The second letter has a special slant, however. It was probably written while Paul was in prison in Rome, awaiting execution (2 Tim. 1:8). Here the apostle to the Gentiles records his final words, the most important things he has to say to his most beloved disciple. He does not mince words here. He states candidly what is on his heart, how he views his years of ministry and what he desires for Timothy's future service to the church.

An inductive approach is used in this guide to study these letters for several reasons. One is expressed in 2 Timothy 3:14-15: "Continue in what you have learned and have firmly believed, knowing from whom you learned it and how from childhood you have been acquainted with the sacred writings." Timothy was taught from two sources—from people like Paul and directly from the Scripture. We each have an obligation to have a personal acquaintance with the Bible. The inductive method is used in particular because it motivates personal Bible study. People see that they can understand and apply God's Word on their own. Understanding the Bible is not a magical process. Finally, Christian leaders are especially obligated to have a solid knowledge of the Word.

This guide can be used by individuals or groups. If it is used in a group context, it is strongly suggested that each member have a copy of this guide to record his or her observations before the group meeting and then to note the insights of others. Prior study can stimulate discussion since time has already been spent in observing the basic facts of the text.

This guide follows the text and paragraphing of the Revised Standard Version. Though it is not necessary to use this version, it may be helpful. This is particularly true for the leader of a group. A group may also find it helpful if everyone uses the same version to avoid disputing about words.

The group leader will also want to read the notes in the back of this guide before the study. These give some hints on how to get the most out of each group discussion. James Nyquist's *Leading Bible Discussions* (IVP), especially chapter eight, has other very helpful suggestions for a leader.

All of this will take a certain amount of work and struggle. But such is the task set before a Christian leader, as studying 1 and 2 Timothy will show.

1

A Leader's Motivation

1 Timothy 1

Purposes

1. To understand the proper motivation for a Christian leader.
2. To motivate leaders to diligently fulfill the ministry God has called them to.
3. To reflect on personal goals necessary to fulfill leadership responsibilities with pure motivation.

1. What do you think should be the primary goal of a Christian leader?

2. Sometimes people are thrust into leadership, sometimes they fall into it and sometimes they jump into it. Paul's point in 1 Timothy 1 is that however they get there, they should also be called to it. This study seeks to answer the question, "What motivates you as a leader?" First, read all of 1 Timothy to get an overview of the letter. Notice while you read the different people mentioned and what is said about them.

Now focus on 1 Timothy 1. What does Paul say about his teachings, character and call?

3. Now consider Timothy. Why is he at Ephesus? What is his relationship to Paul? What characteristics does Paul expect in Timothy?

4. What are the teachings and the characteristics of the "certain persons" referred to in verses 3, 6 and 19?

Contrast the results of their teachings with the points Timothy was to stress.

How does their desire to be teachers (v. 7) contrast with the source of Paul's authority (vv. 11-12)?

How does it contrast with the source of Timothy's authority (v. 18)?

5. What leadership responsibilities do you have?

Why, if at all, do you want to be a leader?

What indications, if any, do you have that God might be calling you to leadership?

How could a recognition of God's call to your present position help you handle difficult situations?

6. What is the purpose of the law as stated by Paul in verses 8-11?

How does Paul relate the law to the gospel in these verses?

7. In verses 12-16 Paul describes God's activity in his life. Notice the specific points in his testimony. How would you summarize these points?

After Paul reviews what God has done for him, how does he respond (v. 17)?

8. Compare your experience of God's grace to Paul's.

How does your response to this compare with Paul's?

9. Compare verses 3-7 with 18-20. How does this help you understand the thrust of this chapter?

How would the description of the purpose of the law and Paul's testimony (vv. 8-17) help Timothy at Ephesus?

How are a leader's character and doctrine related?

10. How does verse 5 summarize Paul's charge to Timothy in this chapter?

What must be your motivation as a leader?

11. What steps are you taking (or should you take) to fulfill the responsibilities you mentioned in question 5?

2

Christians in Prayer

1 Timothy 2

Purposes

1. To understand the place of prayer in the life of the Christian.
2. To motivate leaders to spend time in prayer and communicate the necessity of prayer to those they lead.
3. To become examples in prayer now.

1. What problems do you have in praying—either personal or group prayer?

2. In chapter 2 Paul begins to make explicit his general charge to Timothy, found in 1:5. Prayer is the first order of business in leading a group of Christians.

Read 1 Timothy 2. What instructions are given regarding prayer?

3. What is the significance of each of the following words? (You may need a dictionary.)

Supplications

Prayers

Intercessions

Thanksgivings

4. What is the meaning of "lifting holy hands" in relation to "without anger or quarreling"?

How might this apply to your fellowship group?

5. Why does Paul urge prayer for all men? What does he say is the purpose of such prayer?

6. Who are the people in authority over you that you should be praying for?

How do Paul's comments on the nature of God and the work of Jesus Christ in verses 3-6 contribute to his instructions on prayer?

How, then, should you pray for those in authority over you?

7. What general principles concerning a public gathering are presented in verses 8-15?

Consider the differences in public prayer in Paul's day and today. Today men don't usually lift their hands toward heaven and women are quite free to braid their hair. May changes also be permitted in the women's part in public worship if the general principles which lie behind Paul's instructions are not lost? Explain.

8. What characteristics does Paul say befit women who profess religion?

What characteristics befit such women today in our culture?

9. What steps do you need to take to communicate the necessity and nature of prayer to those you lead? (Think this through in relation to those in authority over you, to those Christians you differ with over various issues and to those you evangelize.)

3

Qualifications for Leadership

1 Timothy 3

Purposes
1. To develop an understanding of the qualifications necessary for those who would serve in the household of God.
2. To motivate each person to examine his or her own life in relation to these qualities.
3. To develop a plan for acquiring these qualities personally and for building this Christian character into others.

1. Think of a Christian leader who impressed you positively. What qualities did he or she display that attracted you?

2. Read 1 Timothy 3, noticing the repeated use of the word *household.* How is the household compared to the church?

3. In the three columns below, list the qualifications of the offices of elder (bishop) and deacon (male and female).

Do these lists of qualifications fall into any particular categories? If so, what are they?

4. Which of these qualifications do you have and which do you need to work on?

What steps will you take to develop one or two of your weaker qualities?

Is there an older Christian who would be willing to encourage you in these areas as Paul encouraged Timothy?

5. In verse 13 what does Paul say are the benefits of being a leader?

6. In verses 14-15 what does Paul say is his purpose in writing the letter?

How would these instructions affect Timothy's behavior in the household of God?

7. In verse 16 Paul is caught up in worship. The word *mystery* as used by Paul means that which was hidden until it was revealed to us by God through Christ. What do we learn about his view of the gospel in this verse?

8. In conclusion, why is it important for Christian leaders to meet the kind of qualifications Paul mentions in this chapter?

Given your particular situation, why is it important for you to know how you "ought to behave in the household of God"?

4

The Example of a Leader

1 Timothy 4

Purposes

1. To understand the place of sound teaching and sound conduct in the life of a leader by examining the checklist Paul gives to Timothy.
2. To grow in desire for these disciplines.
3. To determine specifically how to grow as a godly example.

1. Do you feel that, as a leader, you are on the spot, that people are continually watching you, evaluating every word and action? Explain.

2. The very fact of leadership makes you extremely visible.

People watch you closely. Your every move is on display—good or bad. Leaders, then, not only are responsible for how they lead followers in particular tasks, but for how they live their whole life.

Read 1 Timothy 4:1-5. What does Paul say will cause some people to depart from the faith?

In broad terms, what is wrong with the practices these people fall into?

---

3. How should those who know the truth differ from those who have departed from the faith?

What things or practices have you rejected which, in fact, God has created?

---

4. Read 1 Timothy 4:6-16. List the exhortations Paul gives Timothy here.

---

5. Let's look at some of these exhortations more closely. To what instructions is Paul referring in verse 6?

Where else in this chapter does Paul re-emphasize this aspect of Timothy's ministry?

6. What is godliness?

How do we train in godliness?

Why is godliness of value in every way?

7. Why was it necessary for Paul to tell Timothy to let no one despise his youth (v. 12)?

How was he to avoid this potential problem?

If people question your qualifications for leadership, how should you respond?

What specifically can you do to be an example to others—in speech, conduct, love, faith or purity?

What responsibility does Timothy have for his gift?

8. How does verse 16 summarize the two main thrusts of this chapter?

How can regularly taking "heed to yourself and to your teachings" (self-review and evaluation) help you be a better example?

What practical steps will you take to become more disciplined in evaluating and reviewing yourself?

9. Self-evaluation is usually not easy. Few people want to dwell on what is wrong with themselves. But if you are to be an example to others, you must know where you fall short. Even with this motivation, however, you may still have no basis on which to evaluate your strengths and weaknesses.

Back in study one, question 5, you listed some of your leadership responsibilities. On a separate sheet of paper, take time to put more detail in this list, to state more explicitly what you want to see accomplished and how you will accomplish it. Be sure to also include goals for what you want to happen in your own life, for growing in personal godliness. Perhaps develop the ways to be an example to others that you listed in question 7.

5

In the Family

1 Timothy 5:1—6:2

Purposes
1. To understand scriptural guidelines for a variety of relationships in the body of Christ.
2. To determine attitudes and actions that need to change to bring them in accord with scriptural principles.

1. How would you characterize the relationships in your fellowship? Businesslike? Congenial? Tense? Nonexistent? Superficial? Warm?

Why did you answer as you did?

2. Read 1 Timothy 5:1—6:2 to see what Paul says relations among believers should be. What are the general guidelines for relationships which Paul has given Timothy in 5:1-2?

In your own words, then, describe how Paul expects Timothy to behave toward older men.

Toward younger men.

Toward older women.

Toward younger women.

3. Why does Paul compare these relationships to family relationships?

Why is the phrase "in all purity" used in regard to these instructions?

How can you live out this attitude in your fellowship group?

4. In verses 3-8, Paul divides widows into what two groups?

Who is to provide for each?

5. Verses 9-16 then consider those widows who have no family to care for them. Into what two groups does he divide these widows?

Who does he say should provide for each?

How are leaders to be treated (vv. 17-22)?

7. Specifically, what was the proper procedure for disciplining those whose conduct or leadership was questioned?

What was the desired effect of this type of discipline?

How should discipline of leaders be handled in your fellowship?

8. The laying on of hands was a service formally setting apart a person for a particular ministry (see 1 Tim. 4:14 and 2 Tim. 1:6). Why should this be done carefully?

How does the phrase "keep yourself pure" fit in this context?

9. How do verses 24-25 contribute to our understanding of choosing and evaluating leaders?

10. How is 6:1-2 consistent with Paul's other instructions governing relationships among believers?

11. From the instructions given, summarize in a sentence how believers should relate to one another.

12. What are a leader's responsibilities in seeing that this takes place?

In what areas do you need to grow to fulfill these tasks?

6

Avoiding the Snares of Leadership

1 Timothy 6:3-21

Purposes

1. To examine the temptations leaders may face.

2. To contrast these potential problems with what God desires of leaders.

3. To bring personal motivation as a leader more closely into harmony with practice.

1. What potential pitfalls and temptations are Christian leaders likely to face?

2. Along with the responsibilities and the privileges of leadership go certain dangers. Leaders need to be warned of these so they will be able to recognize them and muster resources against them when they arise.

Read 1 Timothy 6:3-21 looking especially for the dangers leaders can face. What characterizes false teachers? What motivates them?

---

3. In contrast, what should motivate a Christian leader?

What else should characterize the man of God?

---

4. List the verbs Paul uses in verses 11-14, 20-21.

What would this communicate to you if you received this letter?

How seriously do you take the responsibilities God has entrusted to you?

What are the dangers of not taking leadership seriously?

5. What are the dangers of desiring material gain?

Contrast what Paul says about those who desire riches (vv. 3-10) with what he says about the rich (vv. 17-19).

6. Is it possible for material benefits to warp our perspective on the Christian life? How? Why?

In what ways do your attitudes and responses to material wealth need to be changed?

What other specific things could falsely motivate you as a Christian leader?

7. How does a leader's motivation relate to the results of his work?

8. How do verses 20-21 summarize the concerns Paul has expressed throughout this letter?

Spend time in confession and thanks to God.

7

Encouraging Growth

2 Timothy 1

Purposes
1. To see how Paul encouraged Timothy to fulfill his ministry.
2. To desire to be an encouragement to others in their Christian lives.
3. To decide what specific steps to take encouraging one person for whom God has given you spiritual responsibility.

1. Read through all of 2 Timothy to get a sweep of the letter.
Now focus on chapter 1. Who has helped you and how has that person helped you to grow as a Christian?

2. From verses 1-2, what kind of relationship did Paul have with Timothy?

3. What does Paul say he remembers?

What significance would these events have for Timothy?

4. What are some main events in your spiritual history?

How does recalling these events affect you?

5. Having recalled Timothy's spiritual history, Paul then reminds Timothy to do what?

What is this gift?

6. Why does Paul find it necessary to encourage Timothy to fan this gift into flame?

How can we explain this timid spirit in one who had received God's Spirit and had been placed by God in a significant position of leadership?

How can you help people who are called to responsibilities but who might avoid or withdraw from them?

7. Paul doesn't allow Timothy to continue in his fearful disposition. How does he encourage Timothy (v. 7)?

How can each quality that God has given affect one's life? First, a spirit of power?

Next, a spirit of love?

And last, a spirit of self-control?

8. What does Paul say God has done in his and Timothy's lives (vv. 8-14)?

How does Paul say he is an example for Timothy?

What does Paul mean by, "Follow the pattern of the sound words which you have heard from me"?

How would verses 8-14 help Timothy to not be ashamed of the gospel?

9. In verses 15-18, why does Paul mention those who turned away from him?

What effect would Onesiphorus' example probably have on Timothy?

---

10. Summarize the different means Paul used in this chapter to encourage Timothy to fulfill his ministry.

Consider the practical aspects of encouraging one person in whose life God has used you in the past. Think through and write down his or her needs first. Then indicate what steps you can take to encourage that person's growth.

8

Training Leaders

2 Timothy 2:1-19

Purposes
1. To understand the principles Paul gives Timothy for training others in the Christian faith.
2. To desire the quality of life necessary to effectively train others.
3. To decide how to begin building in another person's life.

1. After presenting many facts to encourage Timothy (his faith, his family's faith, his gift, the glory of the gospel, the faithfulness of Onesiphorus), Paul presents Jesus Christ as the final and most important encouragement in a leader's ministry.

Read 2 Timothy 2:1-19 looking for facts about Jesus Christ which will encourage Timothy in his ministry. List what you find.

2. What instructions does Paul give Timothy in verses 1-8?

3. What characteristics do a good soldier, an athlete and a farmer have in common?

How do circumstances affect their activity?

What are the results of being a good soldier, athlete or farmer?

4. Discuss the meaning of "rightly handling the word of truth" (v. 15).

5. Consider the same questions you asked about the soldier, the athlete and the farmer in relation to an approved workman rightly handling the Word. What characteristics does he have?

How do circumstances affect his activity?

What results from being one who rightly handles the Word?

6. What are the results of being one who does not rightly handle the Word (vv. 14-19)?

7. Now look back at verse 2. To what kind of people is Timothy to entrust the message?

How can you determine if someone is faithful?

What will be the content of his message (see vv. 8, 11-13)?

8. List the principles for training others and the personal qualities needed to be a trainer found throughout the chapter. Be sure to consider the significance of verse 7.

9. What is Paul's primary concern for Timothy?

10. Whom do you know who is faithful and open to growing in the grace of Jesus Christ?

How can you help them learn to teach others?

9

Facing Opposition

2 Timothy 2:20—3:9

Purposes
1. To see what attitudes Paul recommended for the leader in the midst of opposition and dissension.
2. To think through the steps necessary to restore others to true teaching.

1. At the end of the last study Paul mentioned those who teach false doctrine in the church (vv. 17-18). In this study we'll see him use a parable about true and false teachers in the house of God.

Read 2 Timothy 2:14-19 to remind yourself of the context and then go on to read 2:20—3:9. Let's break down the metaphor of verses 20-21. What is represented by the great house?

By the noble vessels?

By the ignoble vessels?

What is the purpose of a noble vessel?

2. How, then, should one handle the problem of false teachers; that is, how should one purify oneself from what is ignoble (see vv. 22-26)?

What qualities are necessary for a leader in this sort of situation?

3. Which qualities are you strong in?

Which are you weak in?

How can you strengthen your weaknesses?

4. What might result from these qualities being lived out by God's servant (see vv. 25-26)?

What is the result of repentance for the opponent?

5. Paul goes on in chapter 3 to warn that while some will repent, there will be times of stress when others will serve themselves instead of God. How are these people characterized?

Do these characteristics fall into any particular categories? If so, what are they?

6. Why does Paul end this list with the thought that these people held the form of religion?

Why are they able to “capture weak women”?

7. What similar situations, if any, does your group face?

What other areas of dissension are within your group?

How can these be handled?

If your group is not experiencing such problems, give thanks and pray for God’s continued protection. But keep this section of Scripture in mind if problems do arise.

10

A Godly Life and Scripture

2 Timothy 3:10-17

Purposes

1. To see the value of Scripture in training in righteousness.
2. To be motivated toward a working knowledge of the Scriptures.
3. To determine the means by which Scripture will have a greater influence on you.

1. Read 2 Timothy 3:10-17 noting the references to the Word of God.
2. List what Paul asks Timothy to consider in verses 10-11.

What two categories do these items fall into?

How are persecution and the desire to live a godly life connected?

Why would Paul want to stress this aspect of the Christian life to Timothy?

3. In verses 14-15 Paul recalls how Timothy came to faith. What were some of the influences on him (see vv. 10-11 and 1:5)?

In training others in godliness, how comfortable would you be in pointing to your life as an example to follow? Why is this so?

How does Paul's motivation make him an example worth following (v. 12)?

4. What role did Scripture play in forming Timothy's faith?

What does verse 16 say Scripture is profitable for?

What does Paul then say is the intended result of knowing Scripture?

How does each of the things for which Scripture is profitable lead to this end?
Teaching.

Reproof.

Correction.

Training in righteousness.

5. What is the meaning of being "complete"?

In what practical ways have various parts of Scripture equipped you for "good work"?

6. How is Paul's discussion on sufferings related to his teaching on the Scripture?

7. In summary, what were the two major types of influence on Timothy's Christian life?

____

How should this affect your approach in training others?

____

____

8. How is what you have been learning in Scripture influencing one aspect of your life—in your relationships, in your studies, in your work or in your faith?

____

____

____

____

____

What steps could you take to allow Scripture to have a greater influence in your life?

____

____

____

____

Consider sharing your answer with a prayer partner, fellow leader or some other mature Christian you know. Pray together and evaluate your progress.

11

Finishing the Race

2 Timothy 4

Purposes

1. To observe Paul's summary comments to Timothy.
2. To understand the need for leaders to be ministered to as well as to minister.
3. To review the ministry God has given in order to take steps toward completing it.

1. Here Paul makes his final, closing comments to a key disciple in what is likely his last letter before his impending execution. He is at once reflective and urgent. But first Paul charges Timothy once again.

Read 2 Timothy 4. What is included in the charge?

What is the significance of these things?

______

______

______

______

______

______

2. Why does he make his charge "in the presence of God and Jesus Christ"?

______

______

Why does he include the work of Christ as judge and his Second Coming?

______

______

3. How do you feel about Christ's return? How, if at all, does it affect your ministry?

______

______

______

How should it affect your ministry?

______

4. Why are verses 3-4 included here?

What examples of this happening today can you think of?

5. How does Paul feel at the end of his life regarding his ministry as expressed in verses 6-8?

How do you suppose these verses affected Timothy?

How does this paragraph relate to Paul's previous charge?

6. What impressions do you get regarding Paul's emotional state in verses 9-22?

How do you explain these feelings and desires following Paul's previous statement of triumph?

What principles for supporting leaders do these verses reveal?

How would the fact that Paul was facing death have contributed to the feelings expressed in the closing sentences of his letter?

What needs do you have as a leader?

How will you meet them?

8. Where does Paul's ultimate confidence and support rest?

9. As you have studied Paul's letters to Timothy, what are the most important things you have learned about the ministry God has given you?

What measures have you decided to take to fulfill that ministry to the glory of God?

Leader's Notes

You will learn a lot about leadership by studying 1 and 2 Timothy. You will learn a lot about leadership by leading these studies too. Leading inductive studies calls for a special brand of leadership. Your task is to be a facilitator. You need not have all the answers and, in fact, are not encouraged to present them even if you do. Rather you are to help the group members discover the truths in 1 and 2 Timothy for themselves. This means you will need to know your material well. A thorough study of the passage beforehand will free you to pay attention to the group members and keep the discussion flowing yet focused on the passage. (James Nyquist's *Leading Bible Discussions* [IVP] is full of virtually indispensable helps in how to do this.)

It is best not to read the leader's notes on a given study until you've done that study yourself. You need to come to terms with the passage on your own just as everyone else does. After doing your own study, consult the leader's notes for hints on actually leading the discussion.

Several purposes are listed at the beginning of each study.

These are to help direct the emphases your discussion should take. Don't be overly concerned if you don't accomplish each purpose for every study. They are not intended to produce guilt but to focus attention.

Most studies begin with a question that approaches one of the general topics of that study. These are intended (1) to create a free atmosphere for sharing ideas by getting group members to discuss something about themselves which requires no prior biblical knowledge and (2) to bring the group's thinking in line with what the passage teaches by relating it to familiar contemporary situations.

Most studies end with summary questions. These usually tie together the main points of the passage and drive home one particular application. If time is short, the leader should move the group to that point rather than let the study stop in midstream. Otherwise the study should be completed at the next meeting.

1. A Leader's Motivation: 1 Timothy 1

If you haven't worked through the study for yourself yet, these notes won't be as helpful as they could be. So do the study now before reading ahead.

Question 4. For verse 20 see also 1 Corinthians 5:3-5.

Questions 4-5. "Prophetic utterances" marked Timothy as called by God for special service. These were to give him encouragement in fulfilling his task. Paul could also look back on his Damascus Road experience as a sign of his calling and draw encouragement from this evidence of God's guidance in his life. In fact it moved him to praise God (v. 17).

Timothy and Paul received their calls in different ways. If God has called you, he has probably done so differently than with either of them—through success in small responsibilities, through requests by those in authority to take on certain duties, possibly through circumstances. How God calls is not the issue here. Rather it is important that there be evidence that God has taken the initiative in your life to bring you to a position of leadership. Looking back on these evidences can be a strong source of encouragement in difficult times, as was true for Paul and as he hoped it would be for Timothy. Keep the attention of the group focused on this rather than on the need to be called in a certain way.

Question 6. See also Romans 3:20; 5:20; 7:7-8. The law made Paul aware of his utter lostness before God and so drove him to rely on the free gift of grace through Christ. That's good news!

Question 7. In the course of Paul's testimony, he essentially gives a basic summary of the gospel.

Question 11. Here is an opportunity for you to help each group member do something which leaders overlook all too often. For example, the leader of an evangelism committee or action group may know the group is supposed to evangelize, but was any thought given as to how this would be done? What goals does the leader have for each member? To know the message well? To learn to care for non-Christians as whole persons? To be able to be comfortable in a variety of situations? If these are the goals (and there could certainly be others), what steps will be taken to accomplish them?

An excellent source book for helping someone to draw up goals is *Managing Our Work* by John W. Alexander (IVP). You should familiarize yourself with this before the study and perhaps bring some copies along for those who might want to read it themselves.

If you like, you could wait to pursue this till the end of study four or emphasize goals both now and then.

2. Christians in Prayer: 1 Timothy 2

Question 7. This will obviously be the touchiest problem in this study. The debate on the role of women in the church is volatile today. And these verses in 1 Timothy are some of the most difficult to deal with. Generally, two lines of thought are followed here. One says that Paul's instructions on women being silent are to be universally applied because he appeals to the creation of man and woman itself. The other says that other things mentioned in the passage were obviously unique to the culture of Paul's day and so the practice of women being silent is also. It need not apply today.

The debate on this issue (and this passage) will continue for some time. In the meantime, Christians on both sides have an obligation to openly investigate positions opposing their own. Where Christians honestly searching God's Word disagree, it is always correct to emphasize the general principles of a passage and reserve judgment on debatable issues. Though you probably won't be able to ignore the issue completely, try to help the group focus on the general principles of 1 Timothy 2. Don't allow the discussion to center on this issue alone.

If a lengthy discussion is required, agree to meet on a separate occasion for this sole purpose and then continue with 1 Timothy 2. Some books to stimulate thought which represent a wide spectrum include *In Search of God's Ideal Woman* by Dorothy Pape (IVP), *All We're Meant to Be* by Letha Scanzoni and Nancy Hardesty (Word) and *Let Me Be a Woman* by Elisabeth Elliot (Tyndale).

3. Qualifications for Leadership: 1 Timothy 3

Question 1. You could also discuss this question from a negative perspective. What qualities displayed by particular Christian leaders (you needn't name names) have repelled you?

4. The Example of a Leader: 1 Timothy 4

Question 2. The "doctrines of demons" (v. 1) are not doctrines about demons but rather doctrines which come from demons.

Question 5. In discussing the instructions Paul refers to in verse 6, you might find this a good opportunity to summarize the teachings of the first three chapters. As also expressed explicitly in verses 11 and 13, and implicitly in verses 1-5, teaching sound doctrine was one of Timothy's primary functions.

Question 9. See study one, especially question 11 and the accompanying leader's notes.

You could make this question an assignment due at your next group meeting. Then beforehand you could discuss frustrations, problems and successes in developing such a list of goals, and try to help each other finish the job.

5. In the Family: 1 Timothy 5:1—6:2

Questions 4 and 5. You may or may not have widows in your immediate fellowship. If you do, application should be relatively easy—in theory. Practice is always tougher. But don't let the group avoid the implications of Paul's instructions.

If you don't have widows, application can still be made. Again, help the group do this concretely. As Paul says in 1 Corinthians 12:23, "Those parts of the body which we think less honorable we invest with the greater honor." Who are the "less honorable" members of your fellowship, those who might seem a burden? How can you clothe them with greater honor, give greater support and care to them? How can they serve your fellowship and thus bring honor to it?

6. Avoiding the Snares of Leadership: 1 Timothy 6:3-21

Question 5. In the Western world the issue of materialism is, for Christians, more subtle than we might first imagine. Group participants who feel Paul's warning here could not possibly apply to them may be challenged by such IVP booklets as *The Salvation of Zachary Baumkletterer* by George Mavrodes and *The Graduated Tithe* by Ronald Sider. For a fuller treatment see Sider's *Rich Christians in an Age of Hunger.*

7. Encouraging Growth: 2 Timothy 1

Throughout the study, help the group draw encouragement in their own lives from the counsel Paul gives Timothy. However, let the emphasis switch in question 10. Having been encouraged ourselves, now direct the group's attention to how they can encourage others to fight the good fight.

Question 4. Remembering is a very important part of a Christian's life. It is a source of thanksgiving. It can also revitalize a sagging faith.

Question 5. It is not explicit what gift Timothy received. However, 2 Timothy 4:5 might give a clue. So might the very responsibility Paul gave Timothy for the Ephesian church (1 Tim. 1:3-5).

Question 6. The intent is to emphasize the constant need to exercise God's power made available through his Spirit. If we are sensitive to the symptoms of timidity, fearfulness and allowing gifts to fall into disuse, we can then know when to encourage such people to preserve their commitment to God and to rely on him.

Question 10. Two cautions for this question. First, don't let the group rush off with practical ways of encouraging someone without adequate analysis of needs. It's like a doctor prescribing medicine without identifying symptoms much less taking the time to diagnose the illness. Second, when you do move to practical steps, try to help the group follow Paul's example of encouragement which you summarized at the beginning of question 10. You didn't study 2 Timothy 1 just to come up with your own ideas on encouragement. Scripture is profitable in many ways, as we'll find out in 2 Timothy 3. Let this be one of them.

8. Training Leaders: 2 Timothy 2:1-19

If you train others, realize that they will follow your example —good or bad. This is the thrust of Paul's message in this chapter. Your character must be strong and godly if you are to be able to train others adequately.

Verses 12-13 can be confusing, looking as if there is a contradiction. This saying concerns the dreadful possibility that we might turn away from Christ. If we do, he will in turn reject us. If we are faithless, he remains faithful to his warnings. For if he did not deny us when we deny him, he would then be denying himself, which the last part of verse 13 says is impossible. (See John Stott's *Guard the Gospel,* p. 64.)

Question 7. Obviously Paul has used the soldier, athlete and farmer to illustrate what a faithful person is like. So the characteristics of a faithful person will be quite similar to what you've discovered already.

Question 10. As the group considers these questions, make sure their emphasis in training others is Paul's emphasis: character. Sessions in "How to Be a Teacher" may not be what is needed at all. Rather, "How to Be Like the Soldier."

Note also that while this is similar to the conclusion of the last study, the emphasis is slightly different. Encouraging anyone in the faith is the point of the last study. Training potential leaders is the concern here.

9. Facing Opposition: 2 Timothy 2:20—3:9

Virtually every leader will face disagreements. Some will be over minor points and others over very important matters. Paul's concern is with false teachers not merely with wayward members or minor differences of opinion. Jannes and Jambres opposed Moses as the magicians of Pharaoh. Now other false leaders were confronting Timothy.

As you apply the teaching of this chapter, realize that repentance may not be required of everyone who disagrees. But in serious matters of the faith, this is a very appropriate response. Nonetheless, the qualities Paul encourages are valuable in handling large and small problems.

10. A Godly Life and Scripture: 2 Timothy 3:10-17

In leading this study, your job is to highlight the challenge that Paul presents to Timothy. As Christians, we are not to know Scripture for the sake of knowing Scripture. Our familiarity with the Word of God is to lead to a more Christlike life. Thus Paul was not content just to teach Timothy the Bible. He lived it for him as an example to follow. This is the challenge that faces all Christian leaders: to be so saturated with God's Word that it becomes a part of who we are and what we do. Then we will be able to stand firm in the face of persecution.

Above all, then, in this study do not be content if the group learns what is in 2 Timothy 3:10-17. Help them grow in living the truths found here.

11. Finishing the Race: 2 Timothy 4

In ways there is little new here. Paul is reviewing his main points for Timothy. Likewise you can use this as an opportunity to review the main points the group has discovered throughout the weeks you've been together. Feel free to refer back to other portions of the letters, tying them together. Being steadfast, enduring suffering, preaching sound doctrine, correcting false teaching—all these are found previously.

But something new is added. A leader is not to be a lone wolf. A leader needs others. Paul is not ashamed of this fact. Help the group understand their needs as well.

for further study from InterVarsity Press